I Looked Through my Window

Written by
Michaela Morgan

Illustrated by
Anthony Lewis

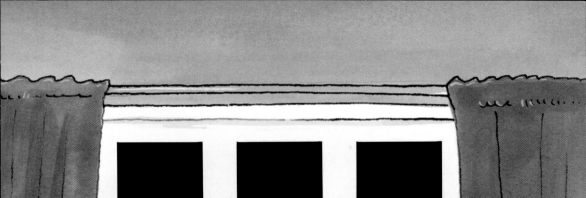

5

6

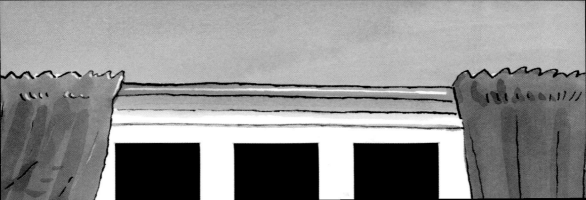

Look in my bed.
What do you see?
Lots of animals,
and no room for me!

I'm squashed!

"Oh no! Oh no! Oh no!" I said.
"There's no room for me
in my nice warm bed."

I stood up tall,
as tall as can be.
I said, "Now then, animals,
listen to me."

"Just go! Just go! Just go!" I said
"It's time all you animals
got out of my bed."

And I mean it!

"All right," said the monkey.

"You win!" said the bear.

"We're sorry if we squashed you.
It wasn't really fair."

"Goodnight, and thank you,"
the animals said.

"It's time for *you* to sleep,
in your nice warm bed."

Sweet dreams!